Little Big Book

COMPILATION OF POETIC
WRITINGS AND MORE

Helen Brooks

TRILOGY CHRISTIAN PUBLISHERS
Tustin, CA

Trilogy Christian Publishers
A Wholly Owned Subsidiary of Trinity Broadcasting Network
2442 Michelle Drive
Tustin, CA 92780

Little Big Book

Copyright © 2024 by Helen Brooks

Scripture quotations marked (KJV) taken from The Holy Bible, King James Version. Cambridge Edition: 1769.

All rights reserved, including the right to reproduce this book or portions thereof in any form whatsoever.

For information, address Trilogy Christian Publishing
Rights Department, 2442 Michelle Drive, Tustin, CA 92780.

Trilogy Christian Publishing/ TBN and colophon are trademarks of Trinity Broadcasting Network.

For information about special discounts for bulk purchases, please contact Trilogy Christian Publishing.

Trilogy Disclaimer: The views and content expressed in this book are those of the author and may not necessarily reflect the views and doctrine of Trilogy Christian Publishing or the Trinity Broadcasting Network.

10 9 8 7 6 5 4 3 2 1

Library of Congress Cataloging-in-Publication Data is available.

ISBN 979-8-89333-894-2

ISBN 979-8-89333-895-9 (ebook)

LITTLE BIG BOOK: Compilation of Poetic Writings and More is dedicated to my amazingly gifted first-born daughter and friend, Takiyah, my loving and supportive son-in-law Stacy, my beloved youngest daughter and protector, Amanda, and my wonderful and talented grandchildren, Jaydyn, Ziyan, Nyla, Zaria, and Mekai.

Lovingly,
Mommy, Mom Brooks, Mama

Contents

The Storm Is Not Here to Stay 1

Jesus, You Are My True Love.. 3

Come, Holy Spirit 4

Dear Jesus, You Are 5

In That Sweet By and By 7

Yielded Will.. 9

Thought—When to Wait—When to Make Haste........ 10

Thought—The Wrong Side of Right 11

Thought—Overflowing River vs. Dry Pond................. 12

Thought—Regrettable 13

Jesus, You Make Me Happy..14

Thought—Dreaming...16

Why...17

A New Beginning...19

Thought—Good Advice 21

My Prayer Today... 22

Thought—Forgive and Know 23

Thought—Past, Present, Yet to Come 24

You Are Not Alone 25

Why I Am Saved 26

Thought—Change 27
Thought—Good Behavior at Home 28
A Short Story—Waiting on Opportunity 29
Thought—God Never Changes 32
Thought—Passion Alone 33
Thought—What Am I? 34
Thought—Eternity 35
Thought—One's True Character 36
Thought—The Solution 37
Thought—My Life Without Jesus 38
A Short Story—Stay Under the Blood 39
Accept What God Allows 43
Thought—Discard and Regard 45
Thought—Making Progress 46
Promised Blessing of Tithing 47
Thought—Unforgiveness 48
Thought—Life is Like a Lesson 49
Thought—What You Need to Succeed 50
Thought—Team Effectiveness 51
The Friend Test 52
Thought—Jesus Promised 53
Thought—A Brain Not Used 54

Thought—Prayer	55
Thought—Declare and Decree	56
Arise and Shine	57
Destiny	59
Mirror, Mirror	61
Thought—Righteous Suffering	62
Let It Rain	63
Thought—Best Year Ever	65
Choose 10 Descriptions that Best Describe	66
Thought—Quite Beautiful	67
Thought—Separation and Reconciliation	68
Thought—Death or Eternal Life	69
Thought—Today	70
Thought—Good Evening	71
Thought—What of Love?	72
The Rain Made Me Smile	73
It's Natural	75
Aging Gracefully	77
Knowing Me	79
Thought—What I Do	81
Thought—Circle of Friends	82
Oh, Lamb of God	83

Twelve Encouragements of Preaching the Gospel 85

Twelve Encouragements for Teaching the Word of God 87

Prayer to Forgive 89

Declaration for Healing 91

The Sinner's Prayer of Confession 94

Afterword 97

Glossary 98

About the Author 99

Scriptural References 101

Preface

The poetic writings that make up this book are the product of over forty years of my life's experiences. Had it not been for the grace of God and the fact that He always helped me through every difficult situation, this book would not exist. Writing poems, song poems, and thoughts gave me hope. Writing was a solace for me, and it helped me stay focused on the promises of God knowing He doesn't break His promises.

Further, my hope and prayer for you is that you will know that God has great plans to bless your life abundantly. Please know you have purpose! You are important to God. You are needed for the betterment of all mankind and the world. If the unique gift God invested in you is not shared with the world, then the world will never know the beauty and splendor it could have possibly known. You are a part of the greatest workmanship ever created by God... mankind. Be encouraged my friend, to embrace who God made you to be and go forward shining your light in this dark world with the gift God entrusted to you thereby helping preserve and share God's truth to a deceived world in desperate need of Salvation. May God bless and keep you now and always!

Humbly,

Helen Brooks

Acknowledgments

Thanks to my oldest daughter Takiyah, for advising me to ensure my thoughts and poems were communicated clearly.

Thanks to my daughter Amanda, for assisting with helping me stay focused on the main goal of completing my book project in a timely manner.

Thanks to my grandson, Jaydyn, for reviewing my writings and giving constructive feedback that prompted the completion of several thoughts that were yet in formative stage.

Thanks to Sumaya, who is like a daughter, for assisting with research, and acquiring various resources that were instrumental in speeding up the process of helping move my book closer to completion. Her labor of love will never be forgotten.

A heartfelt thanks to Trilogy Professional Publishing and TBN for your partnership, belief, and endorsement of this labor of love in written form.

Gratefully,

Helen Brooks

Introduction

The purpose of writing this book is to share the love of God with you through poetic writings, and thoughts that will prayerfully inspire you to know there is hope in all situations. For with God, nothing shall be impossible (Luke 1:37 KJV). Additionally, the book is meant to strengthen those who have become weary along life's journey and to encourage the downcast and/or broken hearted to try again, to love again, and to trust again. It is my desire that each page you read will speak expressly to you and/or your concerns. And that you will feel the tangible warmth of the love of God permeating your inner being, reassuring you just how much you are loved by our Heavenly Father. This book endeavors to comfort those that are grieving a loss, and to minister peace to their troubled mind. Finally, my prayer is that this book will reassure those that are feeling unsettled in their spirit about the frightful world events, and the unpredictable forthcoming storms, that brighter days are ahead for those that put their confidence in Father

God. You need not be afraid. He that spoke the world into existence holds it, and they that dwell therein, in His hands (Psalm 24:1-2 KJV).

The Storm Is Not Here to Stay

Battered and worn,
by fierce winds of the raging storm.
Hold tightly to your faith.
The storm is not here to stay.
You will see a better day.

Ear-piercing, heart-fluttering,
noises of uncertainty,
invade your security,
threaten your posterity.
Hold tightly to your faith.
The storm is not here to stay.
You will see a brighter day.

Storms of life are sure to come,
but this you must do,
hold tightly to your faith in God,
He will help you make it through.

HELEN BROOKS

You need not be afraid,
when the storms come your way.
Be confident and rest assured,
the storm is not here to stay.

Jesus, You Are My True Love

You are always present whenever I need You.
You have never left me alone.
While walking, if I become weary,
You gently pick me up and carry me on.

Your hand never let go of my hand.
Your eyes are filled with compassion and love.
Your strength is made perfect in weakness. (2 Cor. 12:9 KJV)
You keep me steadfast and unmovable. (1 Cor. 5:58 KJV)
As long as I have You, my true love,
I have a purpose in life to fill.
As long as I stay close to You,
I will abide in the center of Your will.

My soul was redeemed on the cross at Calvary,
when you shed Your precious blood for me.
Now I have this blessed assurance,
that nothing will separate me from Your love. (Rom. 8:35 KJV)
Thank You Jesus.
You are indeed my true love.

Come, Holy Spirit

Holy Spirit, I invite You to come.
Come within my heart.
Come within my mind.
Take control of my life,
every day and every hour.
Fill me with Your Holy power.
Holy Spirit, I invite You to come.

Let the old say come.
Let the young say come.
Let the rich say come.
Let the poor say come.
Let all God's people say come.
Holy Spirit, we invite You to come.

Dear Jesus, You Are

Dear Jesus, You are everything to me.
You are the air that I breathe.
You are the words of life that I read.
You are everything to me.

You are my faith,
I walk not by sight.
You teach me to avoid evil,
and to practice doing right.

Dear Jesus, You are everything to me.
You are the solid rock I stand on.
You are the song that I sing.
For in Him we live, and move,
and have our being. (Acts 17:28 KJV)

You are the praise upon my lips.
Your word is forever hidden in my heart.
You are the lifter of my head.
Every day You give me a new start.

Dear Jesus, You are everything to me.
You are the Good Shepherd. (John 10:14 KJV)
You hold me safe in Your arms.
You turn things for my good,
that the enemy meant for my harm. (Based on Gen. 50:20 KJV)
Dear Jesus, You are everything to me.

In That Sweet By and By

I am so glad that sorrows don't last always.
In that glorious morning when I rise,
there will be no more tears in my eyes.
I will forever live with my Lord on high,
in that sweet by and by.

Weeping may last for a night,
but when the morning comes,
we will rejoice to see the light.

Take rest in knowing,
He is faithful and true.
Every promise He has made,
will manifest for me and you.

What a glorious time we await,
entering heaven through the pearly gates.
No more sin and no more shame.
We will be given a white stone and

a new name. (Rev. 2:17 KJV)
It will be worth it all,
when the roll in heaven is called.
In that sweet by and by.

Yielded Will

I yield my will, oh God to Thee.
My life, my hope, my destiny.
I yield my will, oh God to Thee.
To do Your will, I die to me.
I yield oh God to Thee.

With each new day that dawns,
I yield.
And each new night that comes,
I yield.
With joy and gladness, I do run,
I yield oh God to Thee.

My yes to You is yet shaping me.
My yes to You is yet making me.
I yield my will when tears flood my eyes.
I yield my will when pains rip my sides.
I yield oh God to Thee.

I yield my will, oh God to Thee.
My love, my Lord, my Majesty.
For all of Eternity,
I yield oh God to Thee.

Thought
When to Wait—When to Make Haste

There comes a time when one must wait, and there comes a time when one must make haste.
Wisdom is knowing when it is time to wait, and when it is time to make haste. Then, one may act accordingly, responsibly, respectively.

Thought
The Wrong Side of Right

It is not beneficial for one to be on the wrong side of right.

Thought Overflowing River vs. Dry Pond

Why pour water into an overflowing river when not far is a dry pond in desperate need of it?

Thought Regrettable

An unwise decision revealed, and a wise idea concealed is one of the same... regrettable.

HELEN BROOKS

Jesus, You Make Me Happy

Jesus, You make me happy.
I can't help but smile.
You hold me in Your arms
as You would a little child.

I am lovesick.
Your love has captivated my heart.
You are the one in whom my longing soul
is satisfied with, right from the start.

No other can make time stand still,
when we are together, but You.
Only You can cause my cares to disappear
at the remembrance of Your loving kindness,
and Your tender mercies.
How wonderful are Your ways.
Your affection towards me is beyond measure.
Your grace all my days are past finding out.

Gentle yet strong. Warrior yet warm.
You are mine. I am Yours.
Never let go of me. With every fiber of my
being to You, I will cling.

Unwavering, unfailing ever present,
never ending.
Your breath, my life.
Your love, my gift.
Eternal life inside of me. Forever grateful.
Jesus, You make me happy.

Thought Dreaming

When one is dreaming, it is like being the main character in a play which has neither a predetermined plot nor a pre-established ending. However, involuntarily, you are in character-form from the opening of the curtains to the closing thereof. And further, you have no foreknowledge or input as to the outcome of the dream.

Why

Why must melodies have a happy tune
to attract your listening ear?

Why must the sky always stay blue
to bring you joy and cheer?

Why must life have all ups and no downs
for you to know God lives?

Why must trouble never knock on your door
to know the peace He gives?

Why ignore His gentle call
to come as a little child?
You must get in a hurry, your journey is long,
and it just might take a while.

Be not deceived and think you have time
to run, and play, and hide.
Time does not wait for anyone,
and time is not on your side.

Why take the chance and lose your
soul by living a life of sin,
Just as JESUS ascended into Heaven,
He's surely coming again.

You may prepare to go back with Him,
or you may choose to stay here.
Either way it goes my friend,
the clock is yet ticking, the day is ending,
and time for His return is near.

A New Beginning

A new beginning has begun today.
The new has sprung forth.
The old has passed away.

A new beginning with Jesus is fresh, pure and clean.
Its origin is supernatural, powerful and
pristine.

The possibilities are limitless,
as to what you can do.
Have faith in God,
and He will walk and talk with you.

Mountains will be brought low,
and valleys will be made plain.
Instead of drought in the desert,
there will be an abundance of rain.

Thank God for new beginnings.
They have such a way,
to help one stay focused,
at the dawn of each day.

Focused on a new way of thinking,
giving and living,
a new way of sharing, and caring,
moving onward and forgiving.

A new opportunity to show forth His glorious light.
Another day to live holy and be pleasing in His sight.
Thank you, ABBA, for a new beginning,

Thought
Good Advice

Do not make your plans based on what looks good and/or appears to be acceptable on the surface. Consider the foundation, then make your decision based on reality and truth opposed to appearance alone.

HELEN BROOKS

My Prayer Today

This is my prayer today.
Help me along my way.
Unless You guide my feet,
I will surely go astray.

This is my prayer today.
From me, wash all sins away.
Take me and make me new.
I want to be used by You.

Everything that is not like You,
take it away.
Everything I do,
help me do it your way.

Help me to be pleasing in your sight.
Sanctify me wholly,
I want to live right.

Thought
Forgive and Know

When you do not forgive a person that has caused harm and/or has wronged you in whatever way(s), it's like being shackled to that person and dragging them along with you wherever you go. Only after you have truly forgiven that person, or those individuals, will the shackles be broken and your inner being set free.

Furthermore, when you can think of that person, and/or individuals without feelings of animosity or anger, and you use your words to pray for them instead of using your words to speak evil of them or wishing them ill, then you know you have truly forgiven. Congratulations! Now your debts can be forgiven by our Heavenly Father. And He is at liberty to answer your prayers and work on your behalf.

Thought
Past, Present, Yet to Come

That which has been in the past, shall be again.
That which is present today shall be past tomorrow.
That which is yet to come shall yet come.

You Are Not Alone

Your set time is now.
It is time for you to know,
just how much Jesus loves you,
and that He will never let you go.

He holds you safely in the palm
of His hand.
No weapon formed against you,
shall be able to stand.

Love is why Jesus died for you.
Love is why He is here for you.
Love will help you win every fight.
Remember you are not alone.
So be strong in the Lord and in the
power of His might. (Eph. 6:10 KJV)

HELEN BROOKS

Why I Am Saved

They crucified the Lord of Glory.
No greater love is known.
He calls me friend and died for me.
And prepared for me a home.

Where Angels fly and sing aloud,
praises to our King.
Oh, grave where is your victory?
Oh, death where is your sting?

How beautiful are the feet of Him,
whom they nailed to that old rugged cross.
He hung suspended between Heaven and Earth,
so that I would not be lost.

He sacrificed His life for me,
for a debt I could not pay.
Jesus gave to me eternal life,
and that is why I'm saved.

Thought Change

Consider and change the things that you know do not represent you. That is one thing, with God's help, only you can do. No one else can change your ways, but you.

Thought
Good Behavior at Home

Why do you think it is that a child who has been taught good behavior, in the privacy of his or her own home, seems to forget every lesson learned when in a public setting?

_____
_____
_____
_____

A Short Story Waiting on Opportunity

Once upon a time, there was a young lady in her mid-to-late thirties that loved teaching the Word of God. She desired to improve her teaching ability, so she enrolled in a local School of Ministry. Thus, her journey of sharpening her teaching skill began.

Time seemed to have passed quickly. Upon graduating from Seminary a couple of years later, she was ordained as a Minister of the Gospel of Jesus Christ. However, things did not go the way she thought they would. Although she was asked to teach Bible Class and New Members class occasionally, it was not an on-going teaching assignment as she had hoped it would be. Little by little, she began to feel unfulfilled, and started wondering what she could do to change that. In an effort to fill the gap of not teaching on a regular basis, she got involved with other ministries within the church, like joining the praise and worship team, and being a part of the intercessory prayer team. However, nothing could take the place of teaching because that was what she was called and gifted to do.

One morning, while she walked in the nearby park, she prayed and pondered ways she could get active using her gift to teach again. After having walked for a while, she came upon a bench under a big Oak Tree. She stopped and sat down on the bench to tie her shoestring. As she sat down and began to tie her shoestring, a young man approached her and asked if she lived in the neighborhood, and if so, did she know an elderly woman by the name of Esther Garner? Her heart started beating so rapidly until she thought it would explode inside her chest. Her eyes widened with curiosity and amazement at the same time. She slowly rose off the bench and said in a quivering voice... gazing into his eyes, my name is Esther Garner.

The young man took her by both hands to help steady her as she stood there appearing to be shaken at his question. She thought to herself, who is this man and why is he looking for me? But for some odd reason she didn't feel a sense of danger, but rather she couldn't help but notice his eyes radiated with excitement and it seemed he could hardly contain himself when he found out her name was Esther Garner. He began to leap and dance and lift up his voice with jubilant laughter as though he had found a long, lost hidden treasure. He finally calmed down and began to explain to her why he was so excited to have finally met her face to face after having watched her from a distance for many years.

He began by telling her his name. He said, my name is Opportunity. She thought... that's different! She didn't get it until after he finished telling her why he had been watching her all these years. Let me explain, he replied. When I learned, from a reliable source, that you had a gift to teach, and that you were passionate about it, and that you were seeking ways to utilize your teaching gift, I sensed it was time for me, Opportunity, to introduce myself to you. However, since I never saw you up close, I wanted to make sure you were who I thought you were, going off how I remember you looked... from a distance. When I asked if you were Esther Garner and you said yes, then I knew the timing was right for me to introduce myself to you.

The moral of this short story is this, when you think you are waiting on Opportunity to utilize your gift, Opportunity is really waiting on you. Therefore, get busy my friend. Put your gift to work for Kingdom purpose and watch it multiply and be a blessing to countless number of people around the globe.

Thought
God Never Changes

God never changes. Just as He was dependable yesterday, so is He dependable today, and so shall He be dependable forever more.

Thought
Passion Alone

When is passion alone ever enough to bring about a positive change?

Answer: Add an N in front of the word "ever," and you will have your answer: Never.

Thought
What Am I?

I am more sought after than riches and/or fame, but quite often abused more than anything. With me relationships will glow, but without me a true friend you will never know. I have been around since the beginning of time, my value is in-cal-cu-la-ble, but it doesn't cost you a dime. What am I?

Answer: I am Love

Thought Eternity

The death of a man is not the end of a man. The end of a man is determined by the destination
of his soul. Thus, at his end, his eternity begins.

Thought
One's True Character

One's true character cannot be adequately defined by what others think or say about you. One's true character is based on who you are and what you do when no one is around you but you.

Thought
The Solution

When the good of others is not good enough, and their very best will not do, the solution to your situation resides on the inside of you.

Thought
My Life Without Jesus

My life without Jesus is like a melody without words… a song that will not be heard.

My life without Jesus is like a desert without rain… it cannot be inhabited by man.

My life without Jesus is like the sky without clouds… it cannot produce rain.

My life without Jesus is like winning a victory without pain… it diminishes the joy of the gain.

My life without Jesus is like owning beautiful diamond rings… but having no fingers to put them on.

My life without Jesus is like an ocean without water… useless.

My life without Jesus is like having a body… but no heartbeat and no brain activity.

My life without Jesus would be in vain!

For in Him we live, and move, and have our being. (Acts 17: 28a KJV)

A Short Story
Stay Under the Blood

There once was a weary soul in distress,
looking for comfort and a place to rest.

This soul was also seeking for love,
but found only pain.
He had nothing to lose
and all to gain.

One night, the weary soul
saw a sign afar off.
The lights were formed in
the shape of a cross.

I am the one you are searching for,
he heard a voice say.
Ask Jesus into your life tonight.
Only his blood can wash
your sins away,
and help you live right.

The soul felt a stirring deep down within,
a feeling of hope, though yet in sin.

The soul was compelled to turn to the right,
and enter an old church building, but no one
was in sight.

The weary soul took a seat on the very last row,
but heard a gentle voice whisper – closer you must go.

Never having experienced a divine presence so strong,
the weary soul was convinced – I must go on.

After moving to the front row of the empty church,
a bright light shinned all inside.
The same voice so lovingly replied,

Come unto me, all you that labor and are heavy laden,
and I will give you rest. (Matt.11:28 KJV)
[As the weary soul listened intensely, it felt as though
a weight had been lifted from off his shoulders.]
[The comforting voice continued,]
Take my yoke upon you, and learn of me;
for I am meek and lowly in heart:
and you shall find rest unto your souls. (Matt. 11:29 KJV)

For my yoke is easy, and my burden is light. (Matt. 11:30 KJV)

Shaking and trembling, the weary soul fell to his knees.
Sobbing and crying Father, forgive me please,
for all my wicked deeds.

I repent of my sins on this very night.
I want to be made pure and holy.
Dear Jesus, help me.
I want to live right.

And suddenly there came a sound from Heaven,
as of a rushing mighty wind,
and it filled all the house where he was sitting in. (Acts 2:2 KJV)

The soul started speaking,
in a tongue he knew not of.
Endued with Holy Ghost power,
sent straight from Heaven above.

From that moment forth,
the soul was changed.
He no longer wondered in sin.
for all he had been searching for,
now filled him deep within.

As he left the church overwhelmed with joy.
Again, he heard God so clear.
You must stay under the blood my child,
for judgement day is near.

There is no other way my friend,
for you to obtain salvation, rest, comfort,
and love, but by the shedding of Jesus
sinless, precious blood.

The message in this story is simple and plain.
You must be born of water and spirit for
removal of sin and shame.

Except a man be born of water and of the
Spirit, he cannot enter into the kingdom of God
(John 3:5 KJV).

Accept What God Allows

Accept what God allows.
You will be better off anyway.
Trust Him and never doubt,
and you will never go astray.

Sometimes we all ask the Lord the question why.
Why so many burdens?
Why do loved ones have to die?
Why are there so many worries?
Why do I have to cry?

I have learned to accept
what God allows.
Knowing for sure,
He will see me through.
No matter how hard
the tests and trials,
He knows just what to do.

HELEN BROOKS

So, hello life.
Here I come.
Victory belongs to me.
I have learned to put my
trust in God, and not in
what I see.

Thought
Discard and Regard

Discard the discardable—Regard the regardable—Do not hesitate to do either.

Thought
Making Progress

Making progress is working with what you have until you get what is needed to complete the task.

Promised Blessing of Tithing

You will be blessed going out.
You will be blessed coming in again.

When you give one-tenth of your increase
to the work of the Lord.

All nations will call you blessed.
You will rise above all the rest.
Your vine will not cast its fruit before time.
Your joys will be full of love sublime.

When you bring one-tenth of your increase
to the work of the Lord.

Based on Mal. 3:10-12 (KJV)

Thought Unforgiveness

If you harbor unforgiveness of anyone in your heart, then unity has been undermined by you.

Thought
Life is Like a Lesson

Life is like a lesson we learn. The world is like the classroom in which we learn. Therefore, all who are yet living can contribute worth... whether tangible or intangible to humanity thereby, aiding in helping make life a little less cumbersome, and a lot more manageable, for those that come after us.

Thought What You Need to Succeed

You have what you need in your hands to succeed. Until you use it, you will continue to suffer lack.

Thought
Team Effectiveness

A team is only effective collectively as each member is individually.

The Friend Test How Well Do You Know Your Best Friend?

1. What Is the one thing your friend dreads?
2. What is the one thing your friend could eat every day?
3. What Is your friend's Birthday... Month/Day/Year?
4. How many living siblings does your friend have?
5. What is your friend's favorite color?
6. Is your friend left-handed or right-handed?
7. Where did you and your friend meet?
8. Has your friend ever been married?
9. What is your friend's favorite Bible verse?
10. Where was your friend born?
11. Has your friend ever been out of the United States?
12. What year did your friend graduate from High School?
13. Do you know your friend's cell phone number by heart?
14. Does your friend snore while sleeping?

Thought
Jesus Promised

Jesus promised He would never leave nor forsake us, no matter how hard the test. Keep your eyes steadfast on Him, and He will do the rest.

Thought
A Brain Not Used

A brain that is not used is like a folded umbrella in the rain... useless.

Thought Prayer

Prayer without faith is like faith without works...dead.

Based on James 2:17 (KJV)
Even so faith, if it hath not works, is dead, being alone.

Thought
Declare and Decree

Do not worry... worship. Do not panic... praise. Do not doubt... declare and decree the Word of God. Then, watch His Word work on your behalf.

Arise and Shine

This is your year.
Your set time is here.
This is your day.
Blessings are flowing your way.
This is your hour.
It is overflowing with power.
This is your time.
The Lord's favor is yours.
Arise and shine.

Shine in His glory.
Shine in His might.
Shine at noonday.
Shine at night.
Arise and shine.

Shine in famine.
Shine in plenty.
Count your blessings,
for they are many.
Arise and shine.

There is hope for the hopeless.
There is healing for the sick.
The word of God is powerful and quick.
Arise and shine.

There is strength for the weak.
There is salvation for the lost.
At Calvary Jesus paid for it all.
Arise and shine.

Destiny

I have done a lot of foolish things
I cannot justify.
To try to explain my actions is senseless,
for I cannot truly say why.

How amazing it is to know,
though all the sins I have done.
For a wretch like me, Jesus died.
God's Only Begotten Son.

Many things I have done wrong,
that I did not rectify. The time was there;
then it was gone, with wings it seemed to fly.

Some things I have done, caused
heartaches only for me to bear.
And other things I have done wrong caused
heartaches for myself, and others
to share.

So often I wonder why Jesus died for
someone such as I. Sometimes thoughtless,
and careless, contrary to godliness, for
such He chose to die!

Who am I that He so great ransomed His
life for me? Carried the cross up Golgotha's
Hill and died to make me free.
He redeemed my soul with His precious
blood from a world of sin and shame.
He saw in me the vessel I would be
and thereby changed my name.

No greater love can ever be shown
Then that at Calvary. Now in your will,
help me remain your daughter to glorify Thee.

Mirror, Mirror

Mirror, Mirror in my hand, help me wholly before you stand.

Not my neighbor to my right but make me perfect in your sight.

Mirror, Mirror, I must confess I have not always done my best.

From the days of my youth, I have not always spoken the truth.

Mirror, Mirror in my hand, help me daily understand.

Not to judge or criticize but get the beam out my own eye. (Matt. 7:5 KJV)

And when I finally before you stand, my soul's image will be reflected

in the mirror I hold in my hand.

Thought Righteous Suffering

Those who are willing to suffer rejection for the sake of proclaiming the Gospel of Jesus Christ, and remain faithful to God, will play a major role in the move of God that is getting ready to hit this land like a mighty tidal wave against the dusty banks of the seashore. Changing lives forever, destroying yokes of bondage, and getting the captive set free from demonic powers of Satan. There will be an eternal reward for those that are willing to suffer rejection for proclaiming the Gospel of Jesus Christ.

> Blessed are you, when men shall revile you, and persecute you, and say all manner of evil against you falsely, for my sake. Rejoice, and be exceeding glad: for great is your reward in heaven: for so persecuted they the prophets which were before you.
> Matt. 5:11-12 (KJV)

Let it Rain

Have you ever seen a flower grow without sunshine?
Have you ever seen a flower grow without a little rain sometimes?
Daises in the field lift their heads up high.
Do you ever recall seeing a daffodil cry?
Praying hands point towards the sky as saying,
let it rain, let it rain, let it pour.
When it's over down here,
when it's over down here,
we shall live forever more.

Have you ever been deceived by someone you thought was your friend?
They promised they would stay by your side until the very end.
You felt like your life would crumble and you would fall.
But God stepped in on time and carried you through it all.

Trials are sure to come, but rest assured they will go.
And the pain they caused will only help you to grow.

HELEN BROOKS

So let it rain, let it rain, let it pour.
Let it rain, and rain, and rain some more.
When it's over down here,
when it's over down here.
We shall live forever more.

Thought
Best Year Ever

This year promises to be the best year ever for those of us who dare to embrace, without constraint, the supernatural possibilities ushered in on the wings of faith.

Choose 10 Descriptions that Best Describe...

Choose ten descriptions below that best describe the attributes of love.
If chosen correctly, the remaining ten will describe the attributes of lust.

takes more than gives
fades over time
cast a shadow
is everlasting
immediate gratification
shines a light
is generous
is contaminated
is a giver
is selfish

heals
is true
encourages growth
is pure
seeks revenge
is patient
forgives
wounds
is false
demotes

Thought Quite Beautiful

What is something that may be quiet, is quite beautiful, and can cause death if not properly prepared for, and/or if not taken seriously?

The answer is snow.

Thought Separation and Reconciliation

No one is separated from God without initiating the act of the separation. Yet reconciliation is in the heart of God for any/all that are willing to return to Him.

And all things are of God, who hath reconciled us to himself by Jesus Christ, and hath given to us the ministry of reconciliation; To wit, that God was in Christ, reconciling the world unto himself, not imputing their trespasses unto them; and hath committed unto us the word of reconciliation. (2 Cor. 5:18-19 KJV)

Thought
Death or Eternal Life

The workings of sin in one's life results in death. However, one cannot work to earn eternal life. It is a gift of God through Jesus Christ our Lord, and one needs only to receive.

For the wages of sin is death; but the gift of God is eternal life through Jesus Christ our Lord. (Rom. 6:23 KJV)

Thought Today

Today is here to do with it what you will. What will that be and what will it see, that will exemplify who you are? Spend it well and spend it wise, for today will soon fade away.

What then is left undone today... may never be, for tomorrow is not promised to you,
nor is it promised to me.

Thought
Good Evening

The day is at a close. Darkness swiftly approaches or has already invaded the light. What is done is done. Even that which was done wrong is done, and there is no going back to make that wrong a right.

However, the evening is an opportunity to reflect on what happened during the day. If for you tomorrow does come, so does the chance to do things a different way. Things like helping others when you can and how you can, being peaceful instead of disruptive, showing love instead of hatred, giving instead of taking. Forgive yourself and forgive those that have wronged you instead of refusing to forgive. Repeat these actions each new day you are given. Then, at the end of the day, you will truly be able to say, Good Evening.

Thought
What of Love?

If you are unsure that your significant other loves you and you have a need to know, give it a while, and if it's love, it will surely show.

...and you shall know the truth,
and the truth shall make
you free.
John 8:32 (KJV)

The Rain Made Me Smile

Thank God for the sudden downpour of rain.
It quieted down as quickly as it came.
The soothing sound of the rain,
had a way of taking away my pain.

The water from Heaven can wash tears from your face.
It can take your mind to a beautiful place.
I felt a great relief from the inner pain,
and it was attributed to the sound of the rain.

The message received from heaven's gate
was right on time, not a moment late.
It let me know I was not alone,
that my heavenly Father is yet on His throne.
He sent me word that He sees and He cares,
and all my burdens He is willing to share.

The thing I must do is get out of the way,
 and allow Him in.

That's the only way this battle I'll win.
Next time it rains, if you too are in pain,
why not try listening to the sound of the rain?
So here's to the pain that only lasted for a while.
That's why I say the rain made me smile.

It's Natural

I am a giver not a taker,
a lover, not a hater.
I am a woman not a girl,
been a long time in this world.

I do see color.
However, my focus
is on how you treat me.
So don't prejudge.
Wait until you meet me.

I am not a scam.
I say what I mean,
and mean what I say,
because that's who I am.

The universe consists of magnificent,
colorful things and places.
The earth is inhabited by people of
various pigmentation of faces.
It's natural.

Wouldn't have it any other way.
We help make the world a more
wonderful, grander place to stay.

So, with that being said,
see you later neighbor. Hope
you have a wonderful, beautiful,
colorific day.

Aging Gracefully

As you age, has anyone asked you, why are you so
inconsiderate, impatient, or mean?
At times, it may seem true.
Because of a deficit of graceful attributes,
here is my suggestion to you.

On this journey of growing older,
you must ask God for grace to show
more love and more kindness from day to day.
For this to happen, your selfish ways must be a thing
of the past. Remember only what you do for Christ will
last.

You must realize, the seed sown in the soil of life,
is the harvest that will grow. So, to age gracefully,
there are seeds you must first sow.

If you want to receive a harvest of respect,
you must be willing to sow/show respect,
regardless of age, gender, religious
preference, and so forth.

If you want to reap love and kindness, patience and compassion, then that's the type of seeds you must sow. Lord Jesus, help us sow seeds that will help
us gracefully age as we go.
In the name of Jesus, the Christ. Amen.

Knowing Me

I am beautiful. I am me. I am loved. I am free.
I am intelligent. I am strong.
I am not defiant, don't get it wrong.
I know what I deserve, and that's what I stand on.
If that means for a season, I'll have to walk alone,
then hello season, let's do this thing.
For me, it takes more than a ring.
A ring can be deceiving, just like the giver.
it may sparkle, shine, and even glitter,
but little to no worth, does it deliver.
That's why I'm standing firm on
what I know is true. I know who I am.
How about you?
Do you know your worth?
That you deserve more than you know,
If that's not your story, then you are
good to go. Go to higher heights and
deeper depths in God. Reach back
and help another sister or brother that has been
sorely ripped apart. Help them gain courage to
love themselves and refuse to be disrespected any longer.

Help them to know that God loves them and cares for them, until they become stronger.
Strong enough to look fear in the face,
and let them know they are covered by God's mercy and grace. Let us be each other's advocate until we finish the race. I need you and you need me, to hold each other accountable to be all God has chosen us to be.

Thought What I Do

Because I know my identity, I do what I do, not to receive the applause of men, but rather the approval of God.

When a man's ways please the Lord,
He maketh even his enemies to be at
peace with him.
Prov. 16:7 (KJV)

Thought Circle of Friends

Everyone in your circle of friends doesn't possess the capacity to hear your concern(s) with an ear of understanding, a heart of compassion, and the ability to keep private information confidential. Therefore, exercise extreme caution with whom, if anyone, other than Father God, you share your most intimate concerns with.

Oh, Lamb of God

Oh, Lamb of God, oh, Lamb of God.
Oh, how you love me so.
Before I was conceived in my mother's womb,
you knew the way I'd go.

Not at all the straight and narrow
as some might would assume.
But the way of sin, and hopelessness.
Filled with darkness and gloom.

But, oh, the precious Lamb of God,
whose plans for me are sure.
No matter how conflicting my start,
My end He did secure.

Now I know, He created in me,
a reserved place that only He
can satisfy. Nothing else would ever do,
until I gave Jesus a try.

Could it also be the reason why,
your life is void of grace?
The Lamb of God is not invited in
to occupy His place?

I ask you now, my dear friend,
to give Jesus Christ a try.
I am a witness that He does, and
will, completely satisfy.

You will see, the great love He has for you,
as so did I. But only after surrendering all,
and giving Him a try.

Twelve Encouragements for Preaching the Gospel

1. In the darkest of days, when men hearts do fail because evil corrupts and does seem to prevail. Fear not, be strong, stand firm, preach on.
2. Though the hounds of Hell may threaten your soul, because the good news of God's grace is steady being told, preach on.
3. For God so loved the world, that He gave His only begotten Son… to hang and die on a cross made of a tree. It wasn't the nails or ropes that kept Jesus hanging there, but it was God's great love for whosoever would believe; so, preach on.
4. Though weariness of body may slow your steps, it was never promised that your way would be easy, but that God would be your help, preach on.
5. Preach in the summer's heat. Preach in the winter's cold. Preach until you rescue multitudes of lost souls, preach on.

6. Preach through raging storms, preach through torrential rain, preach through constant heartache, and preach through excruciating pain, preach on.
7. Preach on the mountain top, preach in the valley low, preach the Gospel of Jesus Christ everywhere you go, preach on.
8. If friends become few, and if family do not come home, lift your head, and preach on.
9. Preach until every captive is set free, every sinner bows the knee, and every blind eye is made to see, preach on.
10. With faith as your watchman and Holy Spirit as your guide, you are more than a conqueror and you will make it to the other side, preach on.
11. For victory and not defeat await those who dare go through. Remember, the battle is not yours but the Lord's, it is He that is fighting for you, preach on.
12. Do practice what you preach till the last breath you take, and Heaven's gate will open wide, for this is no mistake!

Twelve Encouragements for Teaching the Word of God

1. By the preaching of God's Word, lost souls may be reached, and by the teaching thereof, Born-Again Believers it keeps, teach on.
2. Study to show thyself approved, rightly dividing God's word. Knowing, some that will hear the truth they've not before heard, teach on.
3. Teach the Word of God in summer's heat and in winter's cold. Teach from the New Testament as well as from the Old, teach on.
4. In the darkest of days, when men hearts do fail, because evil corrupts and does seem to prevail. Fear not, be strong, stand firm, teach on.
5. As it is written, so shall it be, resist the devil and he will flee. You need not fear any threats from hell, for again it is written, and it is well. Upon this rock I shall build my church (says He), and the gates of hell shall not prevail (you'll see), teach on.

6. Teach through raging storms, teach through torrential rain, teach through constant heartache, and trough throbbing pain, teach on.
7. Teach on the mountain top, teach in the valley low, teach the infallible word of God everywhere you go, teach on.
8. Though weariness of body may slow your steps, it was never promised that your way would be easy, but that God would be your help, teach on.
9. If friends become few, and if family do not come home, lift your head, and teach on.
10. With faith as your watchman and Holy Spirit as you guide, you are more than a conqueror and you will make it to the other side, teach on.
11. For Victory and not defeat await those who dare go through. Remember, the battle is not yours but the Lord's, it is He that is fighting for you, teach on.
12. Practice and teach His Word till your last breath you take, and Heaven's gate will open wide, for this is no mistake!

Prayer to Forgive

Father God, I realize that only You can heal my hurting heart that has been shattered in so many pieces. Please help me truly forgive _____ for all the pain and misery that was unjustly inflicted upon me, and upon those that love me. Lord, I thank you for giving me the strength and the willpower to forgive.

Your holy word states, "For if *you* forgive men their trespasses, your heavenly Father will also forgive you: But if *you* forgive not men their trespasses, neither will your Father forgive your trespasses" (Matt. 6:14-15 KJV (Italics mine).

Therefore, I, _____, choose to forgive _____
_____,

for_____
_____.

Although my heart is broken, my spirit is wounded, and my mind is in conflict as I open my mouth to say the words...I forgive _____

_____. I choose to override feelings of anger, resentment, bitterness, hatred and wishing bad things happen to _____,
and instead I will to forgive.

_____

_____, I forgive you.
As a result, I am now free indeed because the Bible lets me know, If the Son therefore shall make you free, you shall be free indeed. Thank you, Father God, for making me free indeed. In the name of the Lord Jesus Christ, I pray. Amen and Amen. (John 8:36 KJV)

Congratulations my friend. If you prayed the above prayer of forgiveness, and meant it from your heart, Jesus Christ has made you free. Stand fast therefore in the liberty wherewith Christ has made you free, and be not entangled again with the yoke of bondage. (Gal. 5:1 KJV)

Declaration for Healing

Lord Jesus thank You for taking the 39 lashes on Your back for the healing of my body... Thank you, Jesus, for letting me know that the work You came into this world to do, on behalf of mankind, was finished on Calvary's Cross.

My healing is just one of the many benefits and blessings You have bestowed upon me, as Your child. I echo Your word in Ps. 103:1-5 (KJV, italics mine): "Bless the Lord, O my soul: and all that is within me, bless His holy name. Bless the Lord, O my soul, and forget not all His benefits: Who forgiveth all *your* iniquities; who healeth all *your* diseases; Who redeemeth *your* life from destruction; who crowneth *you* with lovingkindness and tender mercies; Who satisfieth *your* mouth with good things; so that *your* youth is renewed like the eagle's."

Thank You, Father, for forgiving all my iniquities according to Ps. 103:3a. (KJV).

Thank You, Father, for healing all diseases that invade my body according to Ps. 103:3b. (KJV).

Thank You, Father, for redeeming my life from destruction according to Ps. 103:4a. (KJV).

Thank You, Father, for crowning my life with lovingkindness and tender mercies according to Ps. 103:4b. (KJV).

Thank You, Father, for satisfying my mouth with good things so that my youth is renewed like the eagle's, according to Ps. 103:5 (KJV).

Thank You, Father, for satisfying me with long life and showing me Your salvation according to Ps. 91:16 (KJV).

Father God, I agree with Your word that reads, I shall not die, but live, and declare the works of the Lord. (Ps. 118: 17 KJV)

Father God, I agree with Your word that reads; Beloved, I wish above all things that you may prosper and be in health, even as your soul prospereth. (3 John 1:2 KJV)

Father God, I agree with Your word that reads; And this is the confidence that we have in Him, that, if we ask any thing according to His will, He heareth us: and if we know that He hear us, whatsoever we ask, we know that we have the petitions that we desired of Him. (1 John 5:14-15 KJV)

Thank You, Father God, for I am praying according to Your will. Therefore, I know that You hear me and that I have the petitions I have asked of You. I receive the manifestation of my healing now! I know that I was healed over two thousand years ago. I decree and declare these things, and so they are. I pray this prayer in the name of my Lord and Savior Jesus Christ. Amen and Amen.

Blessing,
Helen Brooks

The Sinner's Prayer of Confession

Perhaps you have never had anyone ask you if you want to pray the sinner's prayer to receive Jesus Christ into your life to rule and reign as your Lord and Savior. Therefore, this invitation is being extended to you to do so, if you so desire. Simply repeat the prayer below and mean it from your heart and you shall be saved. The Bible states, That if you shall confess with your mouth the Lord Jesus, and shall believe in your heart that God has raised Him from the dead, you shall be saved. For with the heart man believeth unto righteousness; and with the mouth confession is made unto salvation. (Rom. 10:9-10 KJV)

Say the following:

> *Lord Jesus, I acknowledge that I have sinned. I repent of all my sins, and I gladly receive Your forgiveness. I ask You to come into my life, and rule and reign as my Lord and Savior. I believe You are*

the Son of God, (John 3:16 KJV) and that You were crucified for my sins, and that You rose from the dead on the third day just like Your word says in 1 Cor. 15:3-4 (KJV).

I believe that all power was given unto You in Heaven and in Earth as stated in Matt. 28:18 (KJV).

I give You all of me from this day forth. Thank You for saving me. This I pray, in Jesus Christ name.

Amen.

My sister, or my brother, if you prayed that prayer you are saved. Welcome into the family of God. Find a church where the truth of God's Holy Word, the Holy Bible is being taught, and the love of Christ is being demonstrated so you may learn and flourish in the things and ways of our Lord and Savior Jesus Christ.

Now go! Share your testimony—what God has done for you—with those that are lost and win souls into the Kingdom of Heaven. Great shall be your reward!

Definition of Repent – Webster's II New College Dictionary

1.a. To feel remorse, contrition, or self-reproach. B. to feel such regret for previous behavior as to change one's mind about it. 2. To make a change for the better because of remorse or contrition for one's sins.

Blessings,
Helen Brooks

Afterword

I trust you enjoyed reading *Little Big Book: Compilation of Poetic Writings and More,* and that you felt the love that went into making this book a reality. It is my hope that your life will be richly blessed as a result of reading this book. No matter what obstacles you may face in life, may this book continually remind you that you are dearly beloved, and that Father God knew what He was doing when He made you to dwell on Planet Earth at this time. May this book help encourage you to fulfill the wonderful purpose for which you were created.

Glossary

Repent: See page 95-97. [CAN BE FOUND IN SINNER'S PRAYER OF CONFESSION]

About the Author

Helen Brooks was born Feb. 26, 1953, to the late Spencer and Leatha Brooks. Her parents taught her to love and to trust God regardless of life's struggles. The lessons Helen learned about the love and faithfulness of God while a child yet remains settled in her heart today. It continuously gives her strength and encouragement to navigate life, and to stay optimistically confident in that which is yet to come will far exceed her wildest imagination and/or expectation. Helen has two beautiful daughters, and five beloved grandchildren. As Helen's parents taught her about the love and faithfulness of God, she in turn taught it to her children, and her children taught the same to their children. So shall it be with each generation, by faith, until Jesus Christ returns.

Helen is ordained as a Minister of the Gospel of Jesus Christ and is a teacher of the Word of God. Helen has served as a Sunday School Teacher, New Members' Class Teacher, and has ministered to the sick in hospitals and nursing homes. Her desire is to comfort the broken hearted and inspire readers to have hope, and faith in Father God.

For more information, you may write:
Helen Brooks
P.O. Box 333
Pickerington, OH 43147

You may connect with Helen Brooks on social media:

- Helen Brooks
- @HelenB93022
- lillightintheworld

Scriptural References

All Scripture Reference is King James Version unless otherwise specified

Luke 1:37	John 8:32
Psalm 24:1-2	John 8:36
Acts 2:2	John 10:14
Acts 17:28a	John 12:32
2 Chr. 20:15	1 John 5:14-15
1 Cor. 15:3-4	3 John 1:2
1 Cor. 15:58	Luke 21:26
2 Cor. 5:18-19	Mal. 3:10-12
2 Cor. 12:9	Matt. 5:11-12
Eph. 6:10	Matt. 6:14-15
Gal. 5:1	Matt. 7:5
Gen. 50:20	Matt. 11:28
Heb. 11:6a	Matt. 11:29
James 2:17	Matt. 11:30
James 4:7	Matt. 16:18
John 3:5	Matt. 19:29
John 3:16	Matt. 28:18

Prov. 16:7

Ps. 46:1

Ps. 91:16

Ps. 103:1-5

Ps. 118:17

Rom. 6:23

Rom. 8:35

Rom. 8:37

Rom. 10:9-10

Rev. 2:17

2 Tim. 2:15

2 Tim. 4:2

Milton Keynes UK
Ingram Content Group UK Ltd.
UKHW030208111224
452348UK00012B/977